Carla Iqbal is an early year's specialist from the UK. She has held various roles in the education sector and finds that the curious minds of children never cease to amaze her.

Layla is one of her five children, and provided the inspiration for writing this series. Carla hopes to inspire children and parents alike in creating a more inclusive world, highlighting the joy, happiness, and unique insight all children can bring.

Adventures of Layla Layla and the Beach

C.M. Iqbal

AUSTIN MACAULEY PUBLISHERS™
LONDON • CAMBRIDGE • NEW YORK • SHARJAH

This book is dedicated to my late; mother, father and father-in-law, all of whom passed away without having the opportunity to meet Layla or participate in her adventures. I would also like to inspire all those couples who are to have or already have a child with Down syndrome to nurture this bundle of joy. Thanks to my husband who is the inspiration for this series and also to all of Layla's sisters, without whom these adventures would not be the same.

Layla was very excited. Her friends have been talking about the beach. Mummy promised to take Layla and her sisters to the beach one day. Today is that day!

What should I take
to the beach?
thought Layla.

Layla had a lot to
think about...

Which clothes and shoes
should I wear?
Which toys do I need
to take?

I wonder what the others are taking? So she went to peek into the big girls' room.

They have big clothes and big sandals…
big towels and big brushes.
I can't share any of their things; nothing will fit me!

She then went to find Mummy. Maybe she could help.

Where is Mummy? Layla looked in all the bedrooms, Mummy wasn't there! "Mummy!" shouted Layla.

"I'm in the kitchen," said Mummy.

Layla went back down the stairs, into the kitchen. Mummy was making sandwiches and putting fruit into tubs. Layla's lunch box was there as well.

"I don't know what to pack, Mummy," said Layla.
"Just pack your backpack," said Mummy.

Layla went back to put things in her special backpack.

This backpack goes with Layla on every adventure. It's a very special backpack, with lots of pockets.

a big zip pocket

a small zip pocket

a pocket for her water bottle

a secret pocket

A big zip pocket, a small zip pocket, a pocket for her water bottle... best of all, it even has a secret pocket.

She held her babies, picked some books, grabbed some clothes…and stuffed them into her backpack. "I'm not sure you will fit all that, Layla," said Mummy.

Layla had to choose. I know, she thought,
I will take one of each!

"Look, Mummy! It closes now,"
said Layla.

sun hat
"Don't forget your water, Layla," said Mummy. "And sun cream and sun hat and sunglasses."
sunglasses
water
"Wow, Layla!" said Mummy. "You did everything by yourself. What a big girl you are now!"
inside
sun cream

"Car is ready," said Daddy. Layla looked out of the window. Looks like we are going in the big car, she thought.

"I can see my seat, Mummy!"

"Let's go girls," said Mummy, calling upstairs.

Like a flash the big sisters were in the car. "Come on, Layla," said Daddy.

Layla holds Daddy's hand walking to the car.
It can be a busy road.
She climbs into her seat by herself and puts her arms through the straps. Daddy buckles her in, nice and secure.

This is Layla's favourite part; Daddy reaches back and tickles her toes.

"All set?" asked Daddy. "Travel dua!" said Layla. She reminded everyone to make a small prayer.

There is lots to see along the way. Whoosh, whoosh, cars go past.
Houses, shops and parks. Small towers and big towers. "My hat is falling off!" said Layla.

Mummy passed out some snacks. Sandwiches, crisps and Layla's favourite, blueberries!
"Are we nearly there yet?" asked Rana.

"Going into the car park now," said Daddy.

"Look! They have my special parking place." This makes it easy for Layla to get out. Not far to walk to the beach from here.

P

Everyone gets out of the car. Maybe we brought too many things?
"If we all pick up a few things, we can do it," said Mummy. Daddy carries Layla and the chairs…and the mat.

Layla loves being carried by Daddy. She can play with the bristles on his chin. It feels prickly but nice.
She tries counting his hair.

Layla takes off her sandals to feel the sand in her toes.

"Come on, Layla!" shouted Rana. "Let's race to the sea." Rana holds her hand and they run off together.

Daddy looked worried. A traffic warden was looking at the car.

Daddy went to ask if everything was OK. Oh, no! Layla's special card was not in the car window.

He looked in the car, under the seats, in the boot. He could not find it anywhere.
He ran to ask Mummy. She checked her bag, Rana's bag, the food bags. Maybe we left it at home? thought Mummy.

Layla and Rana came back with wet sandy feet. "What are you looking for, Mummy?" asked Rana.

The warden is waiting for Layla's special parking card.

Layla smiled. "I know where it is, Mummy."

She opens the silver backpack. Digs deep inside to the secret pocket. "Here it is!" she says with a big smile.

"You're the best, Layla!" Daddy ran back to the warden with the card.

They all played and ate, until is was almost dark. It was time to pack up and go.

"Don't leave any litter, girls," said Daddy.

Thanks to Layla's secret pocket, it was a nice day at the beach.

Layla got in her car seat first. She was already asleep by the time everyone else got in.
What a wonderful day!

THE END